THE UNDISPUTED

THE UNFATHOMABLE LAWS OF SUCCESS

Law 1: ***MASTER THE LAW OF ATTRACTION***

Success is in its morphology a naturally dictated phenomenon. This means that you need to unlock the limited perception that you have towards attaining success and wealth. In order for you to attain a level of success in any area, you need to achieve that which you want, and for you to achieve what you want, you need to come up with thoughts of how you are going to conquer, at all odds anything, to achieve whatever you are planning to achieve. Therefore, the key subject here is that you have to think and attract your breakthrough by the particular thoughts that come into your mind as solutions for success to be possible. First of all, you need to understand that you can attract unlimited success in your field by applying the Law of attraction. This law allows us to attract experiences and situations in our lives by our thoughts; be it happiness, good health, wealth, power and also the negative things which may include misery, failure, diseases and scarcity. This law is definite, meaning that it can't distinguish between negative and positive attributes when in play.

In many religions it is believed that 'God' created man in his own image which implies that man possesses the power to create and command things to existence. Human beings can summon the kinds of things they want through their thoughts. This is evident enough in the numerousthings people have been able to achieve till this day. Science helped us understand that fundamentally, human beings are just 'strings' of particles possessing energy, or in other words we are energy forms and that if we exert our energy at acertain frequency we are capable of producing a phenomenon that constitutes change. The law of conservation of energy states that energy can neither be created nor destroyed but it can be transformed from one form to another. How this applies to human beings is that they can channel their thoughts (energy form) to dictate the setup or nature of the events (result of transmuted energy form) that they wish to occur. Our thoughts are the main elements of creation, like it was said in Rhonda Byrne's book **"THE SECRETE",** your thoughts are the primary cause of everything. The Universe is your catalogue and you have to continuously order it to give to you what you truly desire, which in this case is success. Most of the commands we make to the universe or the thoughts that we bear are made subconsciously from our perspective of events that are occurring or have occurred. Learn to monitor your thoughts and fill your mind with thoughts of abundance, positivity, prosperity and success.

The billionaires and successful people you see today all began their journey by having an inspired thought. They worked tirelessly to make that thought a reality, and they are now reaping the fruits of an inspired thought they held on too. The question you are probably having is 'How can I apply the law of attraction to improve my finances and become rich?

Well the answer is simple; you have to think thoughts of being filthy rich, thoughts of attaining financial success. Thinking in abundance produces a ripple effect that helps you to face challenges with solutions in abundance. In layman's language, you tend to think outside the box. You develop a limitless amount of confidence when going in the abyss or battlefield. Before you think of gaining money or any other form of gratification, you have to think of solving a problem that will earn you money. An inspired thought can be perceived as a solution to a problem or an idea or innovation that after being implemented becomes fruitful (generates income). An inspired thought coupled with hard work, self-discipline, perseverance, and determination is your doorway to financial freedom. The Americans refer to such thoughts as million- and billion-dollar ideas. Your inspired thought (solution, idea or innovation) narrows down to what we term as 'goals'.

To be successful you have to work hard towards your goals. Goals are simply things that you have to get done in order to achieve whatever you deeply desire. Therefore, begin to set goals right now.

Get your journal, diary or a piece of paper and begin to write down the things you would like to see changing right now in your life. Writing your goals down is a very important aspect in attaining success in that it constantly reminds you of what you have to do and what you should prioritize. Do this routinely every day. There is a saying in Brian Tracy's book **"*NO EXCUSES*"** which goes like; 'if you don't write down your goals, you are probably going through your life shooting blanks'. Note down your goals, right besides your goals put a motivational quote to motivate you. Set deadlines for these goals. Put cues to remind you of your goals and assign trustworthy people to hold you accountable once you slip or lose sight of what you want to achieve. Spend time meditating to be able to capture valuable ideas. Stay healthy, exercise, pray and develop positive habits.

We conform easily to a habituated way of living. You should take plight in creating and attracting good habits. Focus on the positives and you will attract positivity and success. Make your desires your most predominant thoughts. Note also that as Einstein proposed that *'time is an illusion, '*we should think of it that way. It might take a short term or sometimes a long term for your desires to come to pass after you have summoned them to existence. The time factor brings in another element called 'faith'. Faith is defined as the ability to believe in things that have not seen. You need to develop an unstoppable amount of faith in what you want to achieve for it to come to pass. You need to eliminate all kinds of doubt because doubt is a negative command to the universe that implies that you are not certain about what you want and it tends to delay your dreams. Doubt only leads you to your doom. You need to be sure of the dream you want to bring to life. And to bring that dream to life you should be ready to stretch yourself by doing those things that you like and dislike but that are necessary to be done for you to attain your level of success. You should know by now that bad feelings of self-pity, jealousy, hatred and scarcity are birthed by bad thoughts, so, eliminate them as soon as they creep into your mind. You should strive to be in the correct environment and work on building a positive mindset. Whatever innovation your mind unveils to you, you can create, provided that you are willing to succumb with the pressure coming from the things that you will be required to do to create it. Therefore, if you are running a business or you have a job that is not letting you live the best life,begin to scout for solutions and accept that you can achieve infinitely. Decapitate and demolish all kinds of barriers that your mind is trying to create, focus more on your dreams than on your limitations and you will experience remarkable results. Set out a frequency that is in line with the thing that you want to attract; is it clients, is it more sales of your products and services or that big breakthrough?

 Begin to work hard in cultivating your field with tools that are within your arsenal for you to have a bumper harvest in future. The more you work on your goals the greater the frequency becomes of that energy you've set out of wanting to achieve your dream.Declare your dreams routinely, tell the universe what you are planning to yield from it, the more you do that, the more you reinforce the energy that connects to what you desire to achieve.

There is a saying that goes 'it is easier said than done', and so I urge you to never lose your passion. Never lose this steam that you are feeling right now. Continue accelerating forward. Build a robust mechanism that will be able to destroy any wreckage that comes in front of you. No matter how enigmatic a problem may seem to be, try to pick up the small particles of positivity that you can fuse together to create a resisting force. Remember, it is better to try perpetually than to quit. Fight using your mind not your hands or your mouth. The greatest empire with the best warriors exists in your mind; learn to use your mind constructively. Adopt the 'Growth Mindset'that Carol Dweck postulated in her book titled **"MINDSET"**, see your failures as learning opportunities. Strive to be unique in a positive and more achieving way. Continue to improve and harness that inspired thought until it raises the bar for you. It is your energy and your frequencies that are your superpowers. Your main motive is to create by thought; similar to the role the gods are perceived to play in religion. You are also a god. Stop limiting yourabilities, set out to achieve more than anyone has ever achieved, the sky is your limit. The Law of Attraction is at your disposal and you can manipulate it in any way that you feel is convenient for you. I will give you a scenerio of when I saw the law of attraction in play. Back at home my Mom and Dad were invited to attend a wedding ceremony, and my youngest sister really wanted to attend this wedding ceremony but was uninvited and couldn't make effort to ask Mom and Dad because she didn't want to seem too persistent or troublesome to her parents and so she chose to make herself believe that she was going to attend the ceremony at all costs. She began ironing her clothes and cleaning her shoes. When she was done preparing she got her phone and wrote this, 'Oh dear Lord please let me attend the wedding ceremony tomorrow' and then she went to sleep. The following morning surprisingly Mom and Dad invited her to accompany them for the wedding, she was so happy. A few hours after their departure, my immediate young sister run to me and showed me what my sister had typed on her phone. I was so amused and perplexed by the power of the Law of Attraction. From then I have made it a habit to prepare for what I want as if it were there this very moment, I make believe, and you should also try this powerful thing. You will be shocked on how you will be able to attract things in your life. Perhaps by now you can identify one or two times when the law of attraction has been at play in your life. Another thing you have to eliminate is doubt, which is as a result of fear. Stop asking yourself how the final piece of the puzzle will be inserted, begin to work with the pieces that you already have. The map will begin to make more sense as you fix the pieces bit by bit. Life is like a game of chess, when playing on your opening moves, you begin to simultaneously focus on your middle game, as you enter middle game, your focus primarily changes to how you are going to transition to endgame. You cannot just picture how the game will end without playing your opening moves and seeing how your opponent responds. So, don't be afraid to start small, bit by bit you will begin to learn what is necessary of you to do for you to reach your dreams.

If you had a really traumatizing experience, begin
to acknowledge that things could have been
worse and convince yourself that you are still
alive. Grab whatever tool that is in your reach
and forge ahead.

Law 2: **Become the Alpha**

To attract unlimited success in your life you need to change your appearance and your mindset. You need to work on becoming an improved version of you; *"The Alpha"; "The Immortal".* You need to own the positive feeling of your dream in your walk, talk, dress code and body language. You got to own it to have it. Focus on improving your self-confidence. Your self-confidence gives you a positive self-identity and enhances your selfimage. What this implies is that, exhibited self confidence coupled with a good appearance tends to subconsciously attract people to you. So,take up this opportunity to consider signing up for a gym membership, practice adequate body language, and improve your public speaking skills. Nothing is more attractive than meeting somebody who possesses all the mentioned qualities. Eat healthy and exercise regularly, monitor your body and work on any attributes that you see to it fit to change. Carry yourself with a lot of zeal and charisma, build a robustly confident posture. Improve your communication skills by having more formal conversations with productive people, make sure to practice euphemism. Avoid using colloquial language most of the times. Begin to network and connect with likeminded people. Learn to control your emotions and be quick to accept negative feedback and move on. Focus only on those things that drive you towards your success and bring to you true happiness. If you take plight in working hard towards improving yourself, it will become a part of you, and you will remarkably be transitioning day by day. Groom yourself to have a high self-esteem, that's the least you can give yourself. You should know your true worth and take steps to get to understand and value yourself more. You are actually worth more than you can ever believe. What limits you is your negative mindset with its constant need for instant gratification and approval from society. We train our minds to think that our happiness can only be derived by pleasing the masses and that if we cannot achieve this then, we are rendered valueless. But the truth is that true happiness lies in our inner being, we can reach to it if we constantly work on improving ourselves. Make yourself a very valuable asset that people will admire. Live a legacy that generations will leave to remember. Explore your abilities day by day, you do not want to die with the regret of not having managed to do the things that you really wanted to do. Your life is your most valuable possession, so, make use of it, and make the most out of your life. Give your life substance and true meaning. Stop limiting yourself and wasting your valuable time on things that you undervalue. Never let your insecurities define you, be very emotionally intelligent. Negative attributes such as rejection, pain and failure are there to mold you and not to harm you. They act as your learning aids, so, you should know that every time you conquer your worst fear you learn and develop solutions. Your overall worst enemy in the quest for success is fear. Fear limits you; it overshadows you from your true abilities. You have to know that at the other side of your fear lays your freedom. Get rid of all the excuses that hinder you towards achieving your goals. Remember that excuses sound best to the person who is making them. So, if you want to become the best version of yourself, you must be ready to go down the hard way. You will be knocked down countless times but don't be afraid to stand up and fight again. Self-awareness plays a pivotal role in life, always be alert of the things that directly affect you, and face them head on. Don't worry, because worrying never solves a problem. Be very strategic with the way in which you approach life. Be very visionary and innovative. Use your intellect to control those variables in your life that seem like barriers and those that you think you can't overcome. You should possess a certain amount of personal pride that should limit you from behaving like the average underachieving people in the society. Frequently raise your standards to a bar that is relatively high. Hard times should serve as an opportunity for you to explore other opportunities. Your doorway to success lies in an adventure of your inner abilities. You wouldn't have learnt all that you know by now if you had remained dormant at one state and position. So, feel free to try new things or improve the things that you already know. Never make a mistake of shunning from an opportunity to learn. Understand that everybody is imperfect and flawed although they might pretend that everything is okay. You should also disrupt any attempts to compare yourself with other people because *'comparison is the best thief of happiness.'* Feel free to ask people around you for information or aid that might be necessary for your success. You can also go further by reading books on success or searching for articles on success. Teach yourself the techniques that numerous successful people have used to climb the ladder to success and begin to practice them daily until you also reach their level. Set your priorities straight and never procrastinate. Procrastination in other events might be in a productive way, like spending more time trying to figure out and plan ways to perfect the of making your dreams possible instead of just executing whatever plan you have right now and figuring out the rest in the way. So, make sure you do those things that are eminent for you to be successful, especially, those that your mind considers to be hard and stressful. Your mind has a default mechanism of wanting to do less stressful things whilst craving for the best conditions. Therefore, you must learn to be tough on yourself and make yourself a master of your mind because every decision you make and everything you consider as a barrier is just a mere perception in your mind. Make yourself the Alpha and the Immortal by becoming an undisputed being with seemingly high values. Take center stage in your life, realize and accept that you are in control of your life and whatever you desire it is up to you to make it available by scouting for it. Awaken that beast inside you and become an unfathomable force to reckon. One other value you should possess is integrity. Make yourself a very reliable person; remain principled at all cost. You should become a man or woman of honor; an upright and truthful being. You should try by all means to be honest to yourself and the people around you. Nurture a personality that is in line with societies morally acceptable core values. You should possess an admirable character. Improve your sense of humor day by day by engaging in social activities. Connect with people, I know that this might not sound easy because everyone out there has got different personalities, but, you should try to create a foundation for commonality by figuring out those interests that are in line with your interests or just looking for people with similar positive interests as you. This does not mean that you should try so hard to fit in, submit only to those people who put in the same effort as you in your relationship. You do not owe anyone much attention if they don't reciprocate it. Cherish the connections that you make, remember that as humans; "United we stand and divided we fall". Do not isolate yourself because isolation is entirely detrimental if you are aimed at making progress. It inhibits you from having a real touch of reality. Doomed is a person who builds fortresses in his mind and thinks he can achieve it all without the aid of people. So, break free of your isolation by finding one or two people that you can confide in.

You can only value others if you value yourself, so, take interest in building your elegance and persona. Make yourself very pleasing in character to people of high value. As the saying goes "birds of the same feathers flock together" and so, if you improve your self-image you will begin to interact with successful people and eventually, you will become successful. Another yet important value is trust. In order for people to invest their time and assets in you, they need to establish that you are really trustworthy. Trust is accompanied by honesty and genuineness. Trust is a factor that ought to be developed by two or more entities in order for their bond to be strengthened. Take plight in guarding your dignity and create a track record of truthfulness so that people can count on you in many events. Become a glimmer of hope to people and they will forever live to cherish your existence. Be a problem solver who creates solutions to societies problems and you will open your doorway to success. Successful people are real problem solvers, they strain their heads daily just to make the lives of people more manageable and they are paid their token of appreciation in form of the wealth that they acquire. So, look around and find a thing that you can change to make the world a better place. To be successful you need to be hardworking and resilient. You need to focus on correcting your weaknesses and reinforcing your strengths. You have to train yourself to go to extreme miles in hard work to get that which you desire. Train your body and mind to obey you just like a master does to his servants. You need to protect yourself from doing what is extraneous but easy and do what is relevant but tough. I assure you today that hard work never goes to waste because you learn a lot of principles from working hard. Regardless of the turn-out of the goal you are working hard for, you learn; creativity, how to be more productive, self-discipline and mastery. To be honest the only thing you would have lost by working hard and not achieving your goal is time which is merely an illusion because you still have multiple doors to explore and, in some cases, you can still try with more strength to achieve that goal. Whenever you face a drawback, you need to be able to bounce back.

LAW 3: **The Law of Action**

This law is also known as the 'law of cause and effect', it is similar to Sir Isaac Newton's third law of motion which states that 'to every acting force there is an equal but opposite reacting force'. It states that to whatever actions and decisions you make, there will be results and consequences. In other terms you reap what you have sown. So, whatever you are going through right now, (good or bad) is as a result of your past actions. If you are going through a terrible phase right now, it might be that you fumbled somewhere in the past or you did not take responsibility for a situation when you were required to act. Begin to take responsibility for your life. The best part is that you can change your future right this moment by taking positive well-calculated actions to make you successful in future. I know that the Law of Cause and Effect might be a bitter pill to swallow, but the sooner you get hold of it, the better. Most of the barriers in our lives that limit us from attaining a level of success are created by the mind when it continues to restore itself to its default mechanism of craving for what is easy or expedient. We term such barriers as psychological barriers; they are often due to social factors borne due to perceptions of events that had occurred in the past that we were definitely not pleased with and would like to avoid in the future. These may include things like rejection, dissonance and negative commentary from people that might propel us to feel uncomfortable and give up on working towards our goals. We are naturally people pleasers and we crave appreciation from people such that if we don't get it or if we are undermined by society, we tend to avoid being judged by society. There is a notion in our heads that makes us feel that people's negative opinions have an impact on our lives. It arises from us being emotional creatures, whatever negative feedback we get tends to distort our emotions, and we feel conflicted. But to tell you the truth, all this warfare starts and ends in your mind. In reality without the emotional baggage; without paying any radical attention to what people say, you can do literally anything you feel like doing. To be successful you need to withdraw from being a pleaser of the masses and get to work with doing what pleases you. Make yourself insensitive to people's opinions, do the dirty work that will help you climb up the ladder to success. You have to work tirelessly on each goal you set and never lose your focus. Never be afraid to start small because of fear of propaganda and negative commentary. Remember that your life is owned by one person; which is you and the rest is irrelevant. Rest only when you are done with the daily targets that you have set. Opportunities are always there, it is just that we are too selective and we never want to swallow our pride and do what is necessary for us to grab our dreams. It is only when you reach at the level of having enough self-confidence to do what is right that you will begin to make significant progress towards success. This feature is what is referred to as self-discipline. It is what our colleagues in the military possess. You should have a similar amount of discipline that these people possess. Avoid giving excuses; because excuses delay you from achieving your goals and make you lose your drive and steam. Idris Alba, a famous actor quoted this on excuses, "excuses sound best to the person that is making them up", which is very true because excuses make us feel as though we still have ample time of which it is not only time that is a factor but also our drive to do things efficiently and effectively. Try as much as possible to do things on time without second thinking or making extraneous analysis. Pick yourself up from this dormant stage or enigmatic situation you are in and continue driving yourself forward. Life is too short for you to waste your time worrying and making excuses. You will never realize this incredible opportunity until it's gone. Begin to try by all means to make your life complete. Build a Utopia of abundance and prosperity. A poet named Rudy Fransisco quoted this;

"Muscle is created by repeatedly lifting things that are meant to weigh us down, so, when your

shoulders feel heavy, stand up straight, lift your chin hale, go and exercise. Remember that life is a gym membership with a really complicated cancellation policy. Remember that you will survive. Remember that things could be worse. Remember that we have never ever been given anything that we can't handle. When the world crumbles around you, you have to look at the wreckage and then build another one out of all the pieces that are still here. Remember that you are still here, the human heart beats approximately 4000 times per hour and each pulse, each throb, each palpitation is a trophy

*engraved with the words **you are still alive!** You
are still alive! Act like it!"*

To succeed in life, you need to quit complaining
about your life circumstances, and begin to
execute the things that are necessary for you
change your life. Do not allow your mind to feed
upon your limitations. You can only blossom if
you allow your mind to stay positive, especially
during the hardest times. Your mind needs to be
in the correct state for you to be able to work on
your goals. You should make it a habit to act;
without fail, on the things that are in line to your
goals. Work very hard and very smart to attain
and reach the standard that you most admire.
Start by

acknowledging that, nothing comes easy and nothing comes on a silver plate. Learn to work with the things you have and never excuse working on the targets that you've set because of the things that you don't have. Don't listen to your mind when it wants you to give up on the opportunities that you possess because of some abstract limitation. What we define as limitations to goals in this era are normally factors that affect our social setup. Therefore, you need to disengage from subjecting yourself to those social ethics that limit you from working on your goals. Don't second think when it comes to getting yourself to work on your goals, program yourself like a robot and just do it when you are required to. Sometimes, your actions might seem unnecessary to your dreams when you are working on them continuously but aren't achieving anything yet. Do not give up, getting to your dreams though hard work requires of you to be patient and very disciplined. Whenever you feel the nudge to question yourself as to why nothing seems to be working out, just know that you are about to sabotage yourself. So, before you question, take time to explore new methods or try out alternative activities. Continue working hard and do as many things as you can in the most efficient way possible. Give yourself more tasks day by day. Stay strong and healthy; be vigilant as much as possible. Don't let your gadgets distract you, either find a way to use them productively or pack them when you begin your work. Find a productive recreation that best suits your personality and begin to practice it daily at your leisure time. Your free time should be as limited as possible; meaning that majority of your time should be utilized doing productive things. Your free time should only constitute time to eat, sleep, network and participate in a recreation. Use your mind and your body to break the barriers in your life. Get yourself out of that ditch that you are trapped in. Self-pity and laziness will only prolong the days that you will stay in that ditch of failure. Failure makes you feel derailed because we as human beings have been designed to live as comfortable as possible in the very best conditions. So, make it your everyday target to restore your life to a dimension that will be best suitable to accommodate your minds' and bodies design. Work relentlessly to break free of the chains that are surrounding you. Apply unlimited effort to improve yourself because self-improvement will help you develop a wonderful amount of strength that will help you break loose of your barriers. You are a very special and intelligent being that must not subject itself to self-destructive habits. Be persistent in finding out where your abilities can take you. Let this be a wakeup call for you to realize that you are forever in a boxing ring with your problems, so it is either you allow them to have the best of you by practicing self-sabotaging habits or you knock them down by working hard on improving yourself. Equip yourself with skills, knowledge and wisdom; these three will act as armor for you in the battlefield of life. Your hard work, zeal, discipline and most importantly, you dream, are what act as your sword. Therefore, carry your full armor daily and find ways to defeat your enemy which is failure and underachievement for you to achieve success. You certainly possess the power to change your life, you just need to be willing to get out of your comfort zone. Don't allow your mind to create a habitat in a position that you are not impressed with, shift yourself to a place that satisfies you, that makes you the best able person. You are constantly growing and evolving, therefore, you must choose the direction you would like your changes to drive you too. Success is a prize for full-timers, people who are willing to go all the way to change their destiny. You must be willing to withstand the pain even if it becomes excruciating and you must be willing to take all the risks necessary for you to reach your desired level. With every activity that you do, take time to ask yourself how that activity is productive or in line with your targets, if it is not, and it is just there to provide some form of gratification, ditch as soon as possible and find something productive to do. Another thing is that you should develop so much pleasure in trying out those things that that might be additional to driving you forward even though you feel you don't have the capacity to do them. Yes, you might fail terribly at first and suck at them, but every failure is actually a roadmap to you succeeding in learning. Failure is an effective learning tool; it helps you distinguish between what is right and wrong, and what you should do or not do. As human beings, we've been naturally designed to feel that we are always right; therefore, failure often triggers a negative response within us that is coupled with feelings of disappointments, worries, grief, anger and unworthiness due to our unwillingness to accept that we are wrong. If only we would accept this component and begin to work on it immediately, we would achieve endlessly. So, whenever you fail at something you've put your physical and mental effort to, go back to the drawing board and formulate new methods to use when approaching it in that area. Failure is not your enemy,it is your eye opener, it shows you where you have loopholes and you have the task to fix them.

When you face your failures, you improve your agility and make yourself resilient to those failures that you have faced. Our life system is more like the model of the immune system in our bodies. If our immune system is exposed to a foreign material, in this case a disease, it tends to put up mechanisms to eradicate those foreign particles. It has to reconstruct itself in the best capable way to eliminate that particle or particles of a similar nature that may attack it in the future. This is similar to what happens to us as humans each time we solve our problems. Our intellect of that particular problem grows and we are more than certain of a way to solve it if we were to face it in future. Your mind commands your hands to do the activities that you perceive as necessary, so learn to summon your mind to exert only productive commands to the activities that your body must do. You should also improve your elasticity; elasticity is what we today like to term as resilience, tolerance and agility. Whenever you are doing something that is uncomfortable but necessary for you to achieve your goals, learn to stretch yourself to accommodate that thing for a longer period of time, do not allow yourself to quit easily. The other very important thing that Max De Pree mentioned in his book, **_THE ART OF LEADERSHIP_**" is that, in order for you to succeed at anything, you must show up. You must be present on the battlefield. You can't succeed by simply coming up with ideas and building fortresses in your mind. You must go out there and begin to execute your goals you must be physically and mentally available for the battle. Without doing this, you should be more than assured that you are heading nowhere and you are heading for doom. Make yourself an action-oriented person. Create a goal tracker that will enable you to check the amount of activities that you are getting done each day. With the amount of intelligence an average human being possesses we have an ability to create innovations and necessitate change where we feel it is necessary. Therefore, take your time to use your hands to create what you want and improve that which does not satisfy you, that is your main responsibility. Teach yourself to cope and accept your failures. Your failures do not define you nor do they imply that you are deemed unfit to learn. They are actually your doorway to learning, what really defines you are your actions. ***"THE BIBLE"*** says that God blesses the works of your hands. This insinuates that we must cherish the actions we take and what we build or what we work on, if we continue working tirelessly without ceasing we will scoop our blessing. You are destined for greatness only that you need to pick up those tools and begin to reconstruct your life. Just do something, do anything, don't be dormant or idol because that is where the self-sabotaging beliefs come from. Our three main weaknesses as human beings are that we like to compare to others. Secondly, we have a shallow approach towards failure, and lastly, our minds' default mechanism of longing for what is easy and gratifying in the short term other than acknowledging and exploring its long-term repercussions. Think-big, do-big and dream-big, that should be your ultimate approach to your life if you want to grow. Come to terms with those events that triggered the fear that you have of working hard in those areas that the mind has deemed impossible or harmful to change. Even if your mind tries to remind you of the event, don't think twice about it and just go fix it. Appreciate your mind for this mechanism that was created to protect you and tell it that you have chosen to go an alternative route. You should realize by this day that you have not achieved anything by following your minds option of avoiding your problems because the truth of the matter is that you have to solve them and they are no two ways about it. Make use of your hands and become a very action-oriented being.

LAW 4: **Maximum power and influence**

Successful people are by far the most powerful and influential people. They are always applying their intellect and influence to stay on top of the ladder. You have to devise a completely harmless way to attain authority. At this point you must realize that your road to success is a battlefield of entities with superior intelligence, honor, creativity and integrity. For you to attain power you must be outstanding in at least all of these fields. You need to take time to understand the psychology of human beings so that you can be able to create the correct baseline in order to attract people to your cause. You need to learn to rule out dark manipulators who are there to draw you backwards or to steal the fruits of your efforts. You need to learn to take control of most situations, especially those that might bring havoc to you and your environment. In any field you will plan to be in, you will always be met with people that are trying to compete for your position or rather the opportunities that you plan to opt for. Therefore, you must find a way to deem yourself more fit than them. There should be an extra element that you must possess to be better than your competitors. In order to attain the necessary amount of strength to become victorious in such a battle, you need to take time to study both your competitors and the people that are in charge of the opportunity that you are heading for. Lastly, you need to gain substantial knowledge about the opportunity you are enrolling too. Then you can analyze the strengths and weaknesses of your competitors and exhibit more creativity in line with their strengths and weaknesses. You must be able minded and able bodied. When you seem to be more organized, creative, skillful, robust and balanced, you appear to be more powerful and resourceful, thereby increasing your chances of earning your much-needed opportunity to reach towards your dreams. As Robert Greene says in his book **_"THE 48 LAWS OF POWER"_**, in order to attain power, you must learn to be a 'perfect courtier'. A perfect courtier appears to be noble and aristocratic, he or she is able to win people's hearts and still be authoritative. You should also hold yourself to a very high level of integrity. Life is like warfare and you must fight both psychological and physical battles that hold you from reaching the top. To be able to win these battles, you must give up that part of you that is soft and sensitive, and replace it with an aggressive "I will achieve it all costs" part. You must understand that most human beings in this era play demeaning and deceptive characters, and they will try by all means to lower you down when you are being productive. We do not like to see people doing the things we have failed to do. This is why you need to be strong enough to withstand all the propaganda and negative remarks people will utter when you climb up the ladder of success.

You need to establish that what you wish to implement is ultimate and true. Being powerful does not imply that you should be hostile to people, but rather it gives you an opportunity to channel down the perspectives of people towards the right direction. It allows you to be more strategic and enables you to diversify the approach towards your goals. When you begin to attract people to your cause, you are able to eliminate the vagueness of your dreams and you begin to appear more meaningful and goal oriented. Power also encourages you to work tirelessly because you will have people depending on you. You will also be able to narrow down your duties by offering them to the people with expertise in that field who are also part of your cause. You should make it a habit to productively network and be as persuasive as possible to be able to make the ones you've deemed fit to support your cause maintain the status in your cause. You must be able to surrender other activities to these people and make them feel a sense of belonging and responsibility. Embrace the talents of the people that support you in a manner that will render you with more power.

Having power also gives you the ability and role of leadership. Being a leader implies that you become responsible for all decisions that involve the well-being of the cause. You become the major driving force of the cause. It also becomes your responsibility to identify those people who seem to lose their steam and develop an interest for gratification. These types of people who Max De Pree, in the book, *"**THE ART OF LEADERSHIP**"* referred to as "people of the dying age", need to be fished out at all cost and recycled.

For those of you who lack effective social skills or have fatal psychological problems that tend to draw you back from networking, I urge you to work tirelessly in trying to dominate your mind because that is where the main barrier is. Defeat your thoughts of trauma and anxiety or do not fear the obstacle that your limiting thoughts set that tends to make you shun away from networking and becoming powerful.

Shortcomings that may lead to psychological barriers are lack of a positive social status, lack of wealth, lack of emotional support and lack of resources. These trigger thoughts of unworthiness and we feel as if we have nowhere to start from but the truth is that it is just our minds playing tricks with us. I know that many of you might come from set ups that might make networking difficult but you should be willing to withstand the pressure in order for you to earn the success you desire. It is only when you become confident enough to conquer the barriers that are in your mind that you will be able to make progress in reality. Imagine having an army of likeminded people who are very keen to succeed. That is one of the benefits of networking and bringing people to your cause. You can market your cause by using modern innovations such as social media, people yearn for propaganda. Market yourself as much as possible to be able to establish more power and influence. Whatever you do that catches public interest must be able to dwell in their minds for a long period of time.

LAW 5: **<u>THE LAW OF GRATITUDE</u>**

There is a saying which goes, *"a person who does not appreciate when given little things cannot appreciate when given many things"*. The key to having more in your life is to be thankful and content with what you have. Learn to work with the resources that you have if you are to become successful. Most of the successful people of this era started with little to nothing in their possession but with those little things they managed to grow themselves. They came to terms with the fact that it wouldn't help them to worry about their limitations but rather that they would use the tools that they had to make things better. Therefore, take this opportunity to come to the realization that you must try out all possibilities and use the tools that are in your arsenal in order for you to blossom. When you are grateful you feel more confident, you feel the drive to achieve more and it becomes easy for you to work in line with your goals. When you are grateful you become more motivated even in the darkest and traumatizing moments because at every point you realize that you are still alive and that you must fight the battle in order for you to make it. In the law of attraction gratefulness is a very powerful tool. It sends out a signal to the universe to demand for more of that which is in line with what it is already giving you. And most people spend their time worrying about their problems and deficiencies thereby urging the universe to bring to them more problems. Therefore, begin now to spend most of your time being grateful for the little things that you have. You can either show that you are grateful by utilizing those little things that you have positively or you can constantly declare to the universe that you are grateful. Make it a daily habit to say thank you or the things in your life just as Rhonda Byrne mentions in her book *"THE SECRETE"*. At a speech given at Howard

University, Chadwick Booseman urged the graduates to "savor the taste of their triumphs".

 It is important to acknowledge the numerous battles that you have fought till this day, and that of which you have emerged victorious. You must appreciate yourself for being strong enough to succumb. Your current image does not define you it is an interpretation of your past experiences and in order to make any improvement, you must begin now to make progress in those areas that you feel left behind. You can only make these differences if you begin to accept and appreciate your old self for bringing you this far and hand yourself over to your new self to take over of you from this point. As long as you don't make this handover; your new and old self will be in constant conflict and you will find yourself relapsing back to your old habits most often. As human beings, we dwell for appreciation; the same applies to our character. We must appreciate our personas in order for them to do whatever we want them to do.   We need to understand ourselves and have a greater picture of our inner desires.

LAW 6 **The Law of Transmutation.**

Information that we receive, events that we experience, actions that we take and our feelings are all forms of energy which tend to cause a disturbance in our minds. Our mind is a system and it has to shift itself and its machinery (the body) in a way that is suitable for it to restore or improve its natural environment whenever it is triggered.

What this implies is that for any form of energy that comes into our system, we consciously or subconsciously choose how to conserve it. We are responsible for necessitating change that shifts our systems and machinery to what we deem as a comfortable or suitable position. We choose how to react to relatively any situation.

So, from this day, whenever your feelings are triggered in a negative way, you should begin to shift that energy which purports a negative feeling or feelings into a positive more productive area, that way you might be able to restore or improve your personal environment.

Whenever you feel conflicted or you hit rock bottom in your life, you should face the challenge. And in other circumstances you must shift your energy to something else that is productive (if the challenge is beyond your control).

Learning to control and channel your energies to the right directions is a very vital skill in becoming a successful person. Successful people always seem to be in control even when they go through the worst experiences. This is because they know how to change their rage, anger, pain and frustrations into a more positive and resourceful product. So, instead of focusing on problems, you should be there using your problems to create solutions. People waste inconsiderable amounts of energy worrying about problems than actually centering that energy to creating solutions. You should have realized by now that you are flawed and there are many loopholes in your life that require fixing. It is so absurd that you should let a single problem or problems define you, when you could actually be out there figuring out solutions. You are in charge of stirring your life in the direction that brings you happiness. Your response (from this nanosecond) to any activity is what will determine your future experience. Make your responses more meaningful. Find as many activities that you can center your energy towards, this will make you feel worthy. Destruct yourself from worrying and over thinking. Be the best version of you and learn to harness your energy. If you become an expat in this area, you become limitless to what you can achieve. Elon Musk, a very rich billionaire who owns SpaceX and Tesla is one of the people who put this Law to good use. Despite the propaganda surrounding his dreams and innovations Musk continues to work hard and tirelessly to improve his innovations. Musk knows no limitation and he has a very positive mindset and attitude. He is currently the world's richest man in 2022.

For you to be successful, you need to apply your efforts in those things that matter to you regardless of the amount of negative feedback that you will be faced with. You need to reach a point where problems and people's negative feedback motivate you to work even harder. To achieve this, you need to drive yourself. The fuel that drives you fuel comes from acknowledging your strengths and weaknesses and then using them to make you a force to reckon.

Law 7: **<u>Law of Mastery</u>**

'Mastery' is when you reach the highest level of self-discipline and confidence that is enough to command events (your dreams) to come into being and also to be in your favor. It is that point you reach when you become numb to emotional, psychological and physical barriers that tend to delay you from achieving your intended goal. This kind of elite feeling normally comes in due to our fear of being average, our fear of losing an opportunity or the complete confidence we have when working on something or an innovation. At this point we seem to have the strength to succumb to anything and the power to overhaul any problem that comes our way. At this point we are able to bend down our life experiences to meet our deepest desires. Even social problems become dysfunctional when you reach the level of mastery. A typical example is similar to the one highlighted by Robert Greene in his book "Mastery" as the feeling you get when studying a few days before an exam. Your mind seems to have fewer difficulties in grasping concepts that you failed to understand in the past. Your mind is able to process information without paying attention to destructions. This level of focus and concentration, this feeling of confidence and zeal that you experience when you are under pressure is what you must learn to develop and harness for you to achieve your dreams. You must learn to endure the pain that seems to be attached to your goals. It is through hard work and perseverance that you can be able to summon mastery otherwise it'll only appear in those moments that your deadline to do a task seems to be approaching.

For you to reach mastery level you also have to learn to fight your inner battles. You must be able to control that inner serpent voice that often lures you to make bad decisions. That inner voice is birthed from your negative habits, propaganda, pleasure and the perception that you think people will have of you. If you can completely neglect or destroy this inner serpent that seems to probe you every time, you will become very efficient in handling your tasks.

You will be able to distinguish between real and unreal barriers that you seem to come across. You will become more skillful and be able to do multiple tasks without coming up with invalid excuses.

Killing this inner serpent begins with as simple as acknowledging its existence and then devising achievable goals that defeat its purpose without paying attention to the plenty excuses that your inner serpent seems to whisper to you. Then commit to beginning your day very early so that you can work on your goals with the best of ease. Eat healthy and exercise to prompt the mechanical part of you. Then take, your time to read books and learn, and lastly, apply the virtues you've learned to express your innovative ability (without ever conspiring with it in any of these stages). Appreciate your existence and declare daily that you will make only perfect decisions. Be like a master to his servants and command your mind to abide by laws. Don't ever let your mind go astray and don't ever let it be idol. Always leave it with tasks to do.

Your power lies within you, it is just beneath you. And if you are willing to sacrifice and work hard, you will be able to unleash it. This power can mold you into what you desire to be.

Nothing in this world comes easy. You must be willing to pay your dues and you must pay your dues in full. You must face and absorb the pain and the suffering that is required for you to get to your dreams. Just continue working, results pop out as a token of appreciation but hard work must be mandatory. You must do more than you did the previous day on working towards your goal. Be fired up and aim right for the stars.

Law 8: **<u>Become a Sculptor.</u>**

"Sculptors" in this case are people that are very innovative and always seek to bring their ideas, creations and inventions to reality. These are brains-on and hands-on people. They love to see their ideas becoming a success. An example of a perfect sculptor is the famous physicist 'Nickola Tesla' that pioneered most of today's inventions. Tesla worked tirelessly to bring most of his scientific ideas to practice. But most of his inventions where not recognized during his time but became fruitful years later. It is very important to be creative because it is only through creativity that you will be able to leave your legacy. Creativity is what sparks your uniqueness and brings out a respectable perspective of you. When you are innovative, you always want to leave a mark in society by creating solutions to their pending problems. The reward that you get is the wealth that you earn after applying your creative ability. Creativity and discipline are what drive people to your cause.

Law 9: **<u>The Law of Integrity</u>**

This refers to our degree of moral soundness. Our integrity is one core value that we should guard jealously because it reflects our personality, thoughts and desires. People judge you based on your integrity and they see you from that lens. Integrity goes hand in hand with honesty because the truth is what sets us free no matter how much pain it might cost in any event. It clears the air. You must not, at any stage degrade or compromise your integrity for this will only degrade and dent your self-image. When people spot your lack of integrity, it derails their respect for you.

Integrity can be spotted in items such as:

(1) *Language*: the way you communicate with people asserts the perception that they will have of you, using the appropriate language,

tones, pitch and euphemisms is necessary for effective communication and indicates a positive moral standard. If you use vulgar language it automatically indicates that you lack proper moral standards and it diminishes people's interest to network and engage with you (especially successful people). Therefore, you should be very cautious with the standard of language you are using for any respective audience for you to maintain your integrity.

(2) ***Level of Discipline:*** this element is the driving mechanism for your integrity. It denotes your robustness, your ability to stay undeformed despite the numerous circumstances, negativity and immorality that surrounds you. When you are disciplined and have goals, it is impossible for people to easily lure you into their dark schemes. You have to stay truthful to yourself and the people around you at all costs. You are always focused on your goals and nobody can shift your focus. The higher your level of discipline, the tougher it is for you to lose your integrity and vice versa.

(3) *Level of Resilience:* you need to be as elastic and flexible, for you to be able to bounce back the times that you are knocked down by life experiences.

Law 10: **Master The Art of Management and Leadership.**

Successful people often take the leading role in setting an example and providing solutions. They are always front liners in solving the greatest problems. Despite taking the lead role, they take plight in serving people honestly, diligently and with much loyalty and respect. A true leader should be a servant of the people. He or she must be willing to put everything down the line to do what is necessary to support the cause. A leader must act professional at all costs and should be willing to make tough and painful decisions when required. A leader must embody resilience and possess determination. They must be focused and passionate about the goals they have set to reach with their followers. Leaders must learn to communicate effectively with their cause. It is through effective communication that motivation and bonding arise from. You must learn to gain favor of the hearts and minds of people that you speak to. A true leader must be willing to make sacrifices for the cause. Tangible examples of items that a leader can sacrifice are time and money. Leaders must also strive to bring harmony to the cause. They must learn to understand and embrace the personalities of the different people that they lead. Leaders must be neutral, they mustn't take sides. A true leader should be able to assign his or her follower with responsibilities that match his/her abilities, gifts and strengths. A true leader must promote unity in the group. True leaders also hold their followers accountable for their actions. True leaders strive to ensure that the environment is conducive for the group members. True leaders do not use leadership as a weapon to frustrate the followers but rather as a tool to empower them and sharpen their talents. A true leader is humble and full of humility. A true leader has a vision for the cause. True leaders talk less and listen more to learn and here the views of the followers. A true leader must posses a positive character and must be magnanimous. He or she must never lose the drive and steam at any point. A true leader is one who properly manages the team. Management simply refers to the ability to effectively run a group. A true manager is one who appreciates the role played by each and every individual in the group. A true manager should also be able to resolve conflict that may arise in the group. A manager mustn't ever pay a deaf ear to the problems brought to his or her table, despite how inconsiderable they may be. True managers are empathetic about their cause such that they seek to create a bond with their cause.

Law 11: **<u>The Law of Persuasion</u>**

'Persuasion' is defined as the communication that is intended to induce belief and action in people. The ability to persuade should be the biggest tool in your arsenal if you are to be able to achieve anything or bring people to you. Communication skills are the number one most effective element that almost all successful and influential people seem to have. If you run a business you should know that in order for you to increase your profits, you need to devise means to attract people to your business; you should become a talented persuader and salesperson.

To effectively succeed in persuading people, you need to dive deep and learn about human psychology. You need to begin to understand how people think and relate to the environment. Human beings are emotional creatures and most of the decisions we make are based on emotional incentives. We make 80 percent of decisions subconsciously without properly scrutinizing the issue at hand. So, learn the dos and don'ts of active persuasion you must align together the traits, interests, and characters of most people to have an insight of what they might seek during an interaction. The key element in persuasion is learning to understand body language. Since majority of the reactions we make to the environment are subconscious, the body tends to accurately portray these reactions without us even noticing. Factors such as facial expression, speech tone, body reflexes etc. are indicators of subconscious reactions, feelings that we don't realize we are emitting out to the environment. Therefore, if you can decipher a human being's subconscious and leverage the knowledge you get to attract people to your life. You will never have challenges with networking.

Law 12: **Law of Learning (*develop old and new skills*)**

'Learning' is defined as the cognitive process of acquiring skills or knowledge. It is through learning that human beings have been able to evolve and adapt to all life conditions. To be successful, you need to use your super intelligent brain to store knowledge and be able to apply it when solving real world problems. Your brain is such a fascinating tool, in that it can improvise and create new features from the tiny pieces of data that you feed it. This really wonderful ability of the brain is what has brought about inventions and innovations that man has been able to create till today.

Learning is the most effective tool that you can use to shape your future (that is if you learn the right stuff). Do not waste your time feeding your brain with information that only degrades you because the mind reinforces whatever information you feed it with, good or bad. Most billionaires invest in learning because it is only through acquiring knowledge that one can acquire freedom and self-worth. They spend plenty of money on books, webinars and seminars because they understand the power knowledge gives them. I made a saying that goes "Discipline gives wisdom and knowledge gives freedom". You should strive to break out of the York of ignorance because ignorance blinds you and creates a substantial amount of fear. Ignorant people even reach a point of being scared of facts due to their lack of knowledge. Therefore, if you want to really be successful, you need to start investing in yourself, read books, enroll for a program and begin to sharpen the skills that you will use to climb the ladder of success. Start networking and learn from friends and people around you those skills that you will find beneficial in order to drive yourself forward. Develop your skills, acquire financial literacy, and read books on personal and mental growth. Learning will make you become more alert and self-aware. You will be able to provide checks and balances to yourself and eventually begin to hold yourself accountable to a very high standard. Learning gives you the drive to build and achieve. I urge you to apportion majority of the 24hours you have to learning. The other really cardinal thing in becoming really successful is learning from people that have already reached the level of success you desire. These people have experience because they managed to defeat all barriers and become successful. Ask them questions or find other means to learn how they managed to get to the top. Do a lot of researching on what you are supposed to do to get to the top. Learn to adapt your body to full mastery. There should be no excuse when a learning opportunity presents itself. Do not teach your brain negative concepts and habits that will harm you in the future. The main skill that one can acquire is that of learning to understand and control oneself. Be what you can be and put your potential to good use. Acquire all the knowledge that you may need to become a better person. You should never seize to learn and improve yourself. It should be a constant process that should begin to feel effortless. Every time you learn a new thing you demolish your barriers and build a new castle in your mind; a castle that you can bring to the physical dimension through hard work, determination and discipline. Be the best learning version of yourself. Learn all the good and productive habits and skills, and notice how brilliantly they will manifest in your life. Become a problem solver, create solutions to problems that are in your environment. Build your environment the way you want it to be.

Law 13: **<u>Law of Investment</u>**

Majority of people lack this attribute. They have dreams but they don't want to invest their time and money in them. They want success to be effortless. They spend all their money on liabilities. They rarely budget and plan. Some plan but give away to gratifications. Successful people are conscious about assets and money. They spend their time and money on executing their long-term goals. They only buy things that are of highest necessity and value in their lives. They have mustered the art of self-discipline when it comes to money matters. They have learned to value money.

Begin now to invest in your future. Don't waste your money on useless items. Remember that this life is yours. Save at least ten percent of your earnings and invest that money so that it can multiply. Your money is a tree, let it bear fruit. Cultivate your field through investing your money in the appropriate channels and be assured to harvest the best results. Investing gives you value it creates a foundation for your life. It pulls the best conditions to you. Begin to practice the 80/20 rule and invest at least 20 percent in every area of your life that you yearn to improve. A 20 percent investment yields an 80 percent success rate. This formula is what is sometimes referred to as the *'pareto principle'*.

The other principle is what I call the *'EB'* rule that I learned from Ebenezer A Odoi, who is one of the best computer programmers of the 21st century. He says that when you spend your money on anything that is not an asset. That items value multiplied by 20 should be what you will be left with. Therefore, if for example, you spend $100 on a watch, you should be left with a $2000 in your pocket to spare and invest. If this condition is not met, live that item alone and start investing in trying to meet this rule.

The profit you make from the investment should also be invested and the system should be endless. Don't hoard money, invest it so that it bears profit. Even the littlest money you have for leisure can be compiled and later on invested.

Law 14: **<u>Be Free Spirited</u>**

Most of the battles that we face are psychological and little do we realize that by accommodating negative reactions in our minds, we attract events in the physical realm. Therefore, it is very vital that we maintain a harmonious environment in our minds. We must learn to spend majority of our time detached from our psychological terror and burdens. At these times we should revive our spirit off of its free will and be able to convince ourselves that we can achieve more than what our limitations allow us to achieve. Raise yourself to a high standard, delve deep into the domain of self-worthiness and self-awareness. Unravel your purpose. Incline yourself towards your goals. Don't concentrate on those grudges that you hold onto or on those events that really tore you down. At this moment, let a compassionate version of you be birthed. This amount of ease is what you should spread in every environment that you are positioned in, especially, instances that require you to network. You manifest the plaque that lies in your mind and spirit to people both consciously and subconsciously. You need to gravitate towards feeling genuinely happy and at peace. Do not compromise your vision or goals by swelling on your limitations. Be vibrant and emit to your environment a positive version of yourself. Learn how to properly manage your emotions. Detach yourself from all forms of negation that hover in your mind. Force your body to start doing something productive in moments of self-sabotage. Never let your mind question the significance of the productive things that you do.

Law 15: **<u>Work Hard To Leave A Legacy</u>**

Your main goal should be to be remembered by people even in generations to come. Your way of doing things and the milestones that you leave behind must be phenomenal. Generations and generations must be left amazed by the amount of the current work you are doing. You must impact the lives of many with the gift of creativity. "You were born here not to exist but to leave a legacy behind"

Challenge yourself to think of how fruitful your existence would be to the current generation and the generations to come. Push yourself in every angle and get yourself to a realization that you are not only alive to please yourself but to be a precious piece to the puzzle that generations and generations of people will be subjected too. Instead of harming yourself begin to work on the ways that you would shape that piece by removing the ridges and rails. The ridges and rails in this case represent your trials and tribulations which are governed by your barriers. Teach yourself to emit love and care to the entire universe. You end up self-sabotaging because you are selfish and ungrateful, but immediately you replace that with genuine love and desire for change and creativity, all that energy will be channeled towards making the world a better place. Get to realize that you have to engrave your name on the world through your input to it. Be kind and very creative and you will earn the happiness and freedom that you wish for. Your happiness lies in providing solutions to problems and making others happy too.

Law 16: **<u>Create A Rigid Constitution for Yourself.</u>**

Most of the behaviors that tend to draw us away from our dreams are animalistic. Our animalistic instincts still kick in and we need to devise very strict ways handle them before they become the rulers and driving force of our lives.

I advise each and every one of you to draft, in writing, a seriously rigid set of regulations that will govern your day to day activities. This constitution should also consist of penalties for engaging in detrimental activities. This set of rules should be placed specifically at a spot where you can see it. You should set a loud timer that will be on, on a daily basis for you to be able to read and counter check if you are indeed following through. If at any point you break any rule and you realize it. Begin to do the task that is attached to the rule that you have broken. Swear to yourself before adopting this set of rules, that you will abide by it. You must abide by each law. This constitution should be the reference point of your behaviors. Create a bond with each and every rule and motivate yourself by recalling the benefits of your following through with every set standard. Improve your constitution day by day by adding more laws to curb despised traits. Be very cautious and strict with yourself like a military personnel. Confront every barrier of your life with this upright mentality and you will notice the remarkable changes that will appear in your life.

Law 18: **<u>Establish Personal Endurance.</u>**

Endurance is defined as the ability to withstand hardships and stress. You must be able to identify instances when your mind tries to lure you to self-sabotage. Endurance requires you to remain firm on carrying out a task or duty despite how uncomfortable it may be. It is this ability to manage and handle pain and be able to remain nonchalant despite the disturbances that this phenomenon brings to you. Endurance is mastering and being able to control the warfare in your mind. The warfare in your in your mind is the greatest conflict that inhibits you from achieving your life purpose or gravitating towards your dream.

The first entity that the mind perceives as an enemy is unfamiliarity. This is because your mind has naturally been trained to carry out familiar tasks and therefore, it makes you believe that happiness can only dwell in the things and methods that you have tried before. But the truth is that your freedom lies in your unfamiliarity. You learn and grow by solving more problems and doing even more harder tasks. You have to break free of your routine and do things differently if you want to be successful. You have to change your overall mindset and your perception of life. You have to stay focused on reorganizing and restructuring your life the way you want it to be. You have to be a bit more tough to yourself and more disciplined. You must be able to get yourself away from any attempts that your mind tends to make to get you back in your comfort zone. Your comfort zone is your destructive zone. It is that area of your life that limits your potential. It keeps you aware from your true value. You can only break free of your comfort zone if you begin to embrace what the author refers to as *productive discomfort.* Which refers to doing things that you must do despite them feeling uncomfortable.

Law 19: **<u>Reinvent Your Perception of Life</u>**

Life is simply based on how you perceive things. Begin to adopt a proactive and positive mindset even as you tackle life activities. Be open minded and do not let challenges confine your space. Become a delighted dreamer, a critical thinker and a high achiever. Do not let your low moments disrupt your momentum. Place yourself in the correct environment that correctly resonates with your energy and ambitions. Meditate upon your goals daily to remind yourself on the routes that you are looking forward to take. Your approach towards life must be one that is filled with direction. Never rest until you achieve your purpose. Establish a firm desire to be a high achiever. Never should you ever settle for less. Reinventing yourself means doing a full autopsy of your character and building a new one that is filled with principles that are driven by a burning desire to be successful. Acknowledge your mistakes and do not deny yourself the opportunity to go through a different route. Begin to realize that you have to hold yourself to a high esteem in order for you to be able to mold yourself into a beautiful accolade or character. Be persistent on your dreams and never let go of the race despite how stiff it may get. Do not compromise your abilities. Your value is unmeasurable. This implies that given enough capacity you can stretch yourself enough to meet any realistic goal that you set. Utilize the power of habit to your convenience. This will help you rehabilitate your routines and your overall approach towards life. Mold yourself into a leader that is filled unlimited courage that is enough to aid in facing any obstacle in life. Never lose faith in yourself. Always trust that you could win any battle that places itself in front of you. Provided that you remain positive and determined on achieving your goals, the weight of carrying the stress appears to be lighter and more manageable. You need to change yourself completely, especially character wise. Adopt a more vibrant personality that is keen to achieving your set ambitions. This new version of you must be one that has totally made peace with your past and must be ready to recover from the past wounds.

Law 20: **<u>Heal from Your Scars</u>**

Wounds can hurt tremendously but it is only when you figure out ways to heal from them that you can make real progress. Healing from life scars is not an easy process; it takes dedication, sacrifice and a lot of ambition. In all, you must find something positive that builds you on a constant basis. Always acknowledge that you have wounds. Don't ignore the pain because when it piles up it can turn into something very catastrophic that can compromise you completely. Remember that the negative energy that you harness towards yourself cannot be exerted on the external environment, instead it only simultaneously affects you the person that is exerting it. Clear out the pride, allow the voices of pain to whisper but gather enough courage to forge ahead. The truth is that life goes on, despite the pain and the calamities. Despite how complex and destructive things are, what truly matters is that you are still alive and kicking, and that you are making every single day count. Learn from your mistakes and never play the blame game because you are only human and you are prone to making errors. Teach yourself to be morally upright and accept the codes and ethics that have been laid down for you to leave by. The further the progress you make in ensuring that every day is fruitful, the more your wounds heal. Your awakening lies in your positivity amidst the darkest moments. Look forward to having a brighter future even though everything seems to be crumbling down right now. Your true worth lies in the nature of your perception.

Learn to handle rejection and loneliness. Confide in yourself more and get to realize that happiness and positivity can only lie in yourself. You can only identify your purpose once you are alone. If you believe in a religion, do not hesitate to spend your alone time speaking to God. Ask God to grant you the knowledge and wisdom to succumb through pain and loneliness. Whenever you feel isolated pray, because prayer uplifts your spirit and detaches you from those thoughts that tend to suppress you the most. Prayer has been medically proven to be consistent in helping devoted people build correct, positive and healthy mental environment.